Severe Weather

Ice Storms

by Trudy Becker

I0895827

FOCUS READERS

SCOUT

www.focusreaders.com

Copyright © 2026 by Focus Readers®, Mendota Heights, MN 55120. All rights reserved. No part of this book may be reproduced or utilized in any form or by any means without written permission from the publisher. No part of this book may be used or reproduced in any manner for the purpose of training artificial intelligence technologies or systems.

Focus Readers is distributed by North Star Editions:
sales@northstareditions.com | 888-417-0195

Produced for Focus Readers by Red Line Editorial.

Photographs ©: Shutterstock Images, cover, 1, 4, 8, 11, 12 (top), 12 (bottom), 16 (top left), 16 (top right), 16 (bottom left); iStockphoto, 7, 15, 16 (bottom right)

Library of Congress Cataloging-in-Publication Data
Names: Becker, Trudy author
Title: Ice storms / Trudy Becker.
Description: Mendota Heights, MN: Focus Readers, [2026] | Series: [Severe weather] | Includes index. | Audience: Grades K-1
Identifiers: LCCN 2025022910 (print) | LCCN 2025022911 (ebook) | ISBN 9798889986294 hardcover | ISBN 9798889986362 paperback | ISBN 9798889986492 pdf | ISBN 9798889986430 ebook
Subjects: LCSH: Ice storms--Juvenile literature
Classification: LCC QC926.37 .B43 2026 (print) | LCC QC926.37 (ebook) | DDC 363.34/926--dc23/eng/20250806
LC record available at https://lccn.loc.gov/2025022910
LC ebook record available at https://lccn.loc.gov/2025022911

Printed in the United States of America
Mankato, MN
012026

About the Author

Trudy Becker lives in Minneapolis, Minnesota.

Table of Contents

What Are Ice Storms?

The air is cold.

Rain falls.

It freezes on the ground.

It turns to ice.

Ice covers roads.

It covers **wires**.

It covers houses.

It is an ice storm.

wires

How Ice Storms Form

Water forms in clouds.

Rain and **sleet** pour down.

Then they freeze.

The air stays cold.

The ice does not **melt**.

More ice builds up.

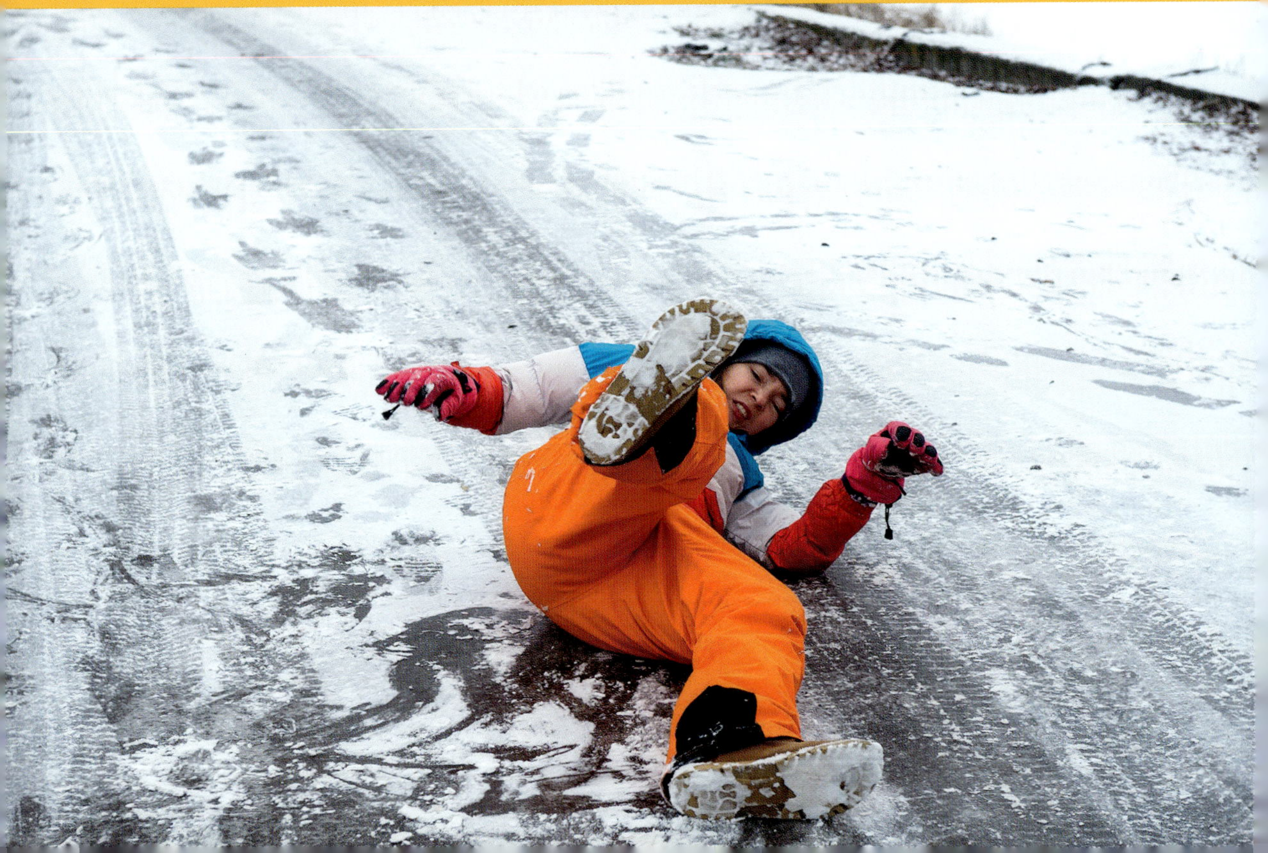

Keep Safe

Ice storms are not safe.

Cars and trucks crash.

People **slip** and fall.

Stay off the roads.

Stay inside.

Wear warm clothes.

Keep safe.

Glossary

melt

slip

sleet

wires

Index